6/08

CR

The Countries
Belgium

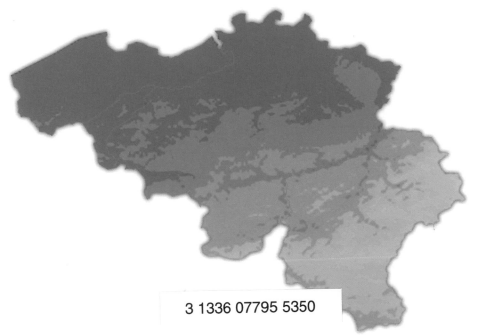

Kristin Van Cleaf
ABDO Publishing Company

visit us at
www.abdopublishing.com

Published by ABDO Publishing Company, 8000 West 78th Street, Edina, Minnesota 55439.
Copyright © 2008 by Abdo Consulting Group, Inc. International copyrights reserved in all
countries. No part of this book may be reproduced in any form without written permission from the
publisher. The Checkerboard Library™ is a trademark and logo of ABDO Publishing Company.

Printed in the United States.

Interior Photos: Alamy pp. 4, 5, 6, 19, 23, 24, 26, 29, 34, 35; AP Images p. 28; Corbis pp. 12,
    25, 27, 30, 31, 33, 36, 37; Getty Images p. 13; North Wind pp. 9, 11

Editors: Heidi M.D. Elston, Megan M. Gunderson
Art Direction & Maps: Neil Klinepier

Library of Congress Cataloging-in-Publication Data

Van Cleaf, Kristin, 1976-
  Belgium / Kristin Van Cleaf.
      p. cm. -- (The countries)
  Includes index.
  ISBN 978-1-59928-780-5
  1. Belgium--Juvenile literature. I. Title.

  DH418.V36 2007
  949.3--dc22

                              2007010177

Contents

Dag, Bonjour, Guten Tag!

Visitors to Belgium will notice that most signs are in both French and Dutch.

Good day from Belgium! This little country is located in northwestern Europe. Belgium is made up of mostly lowlands. As a result, it is considered part of the **Low Countries**.

Belgium's past is closely linked to Netherlands, Luxembourg, and France. This has made language a large issue for the people of Belgium. Dutch, French, and German are all official languages. Today, Belgium is divided into regions that closely follow the language communities.

Throughout history, Belgium has struggled for independence and unity. Despite this, Belgians have created a rich **culture**. Language, food, and festivals are a strong part of the people's lives. This little country has played an important role in Europe.

A boat tour along Belgium's canals is a delightful way to see the country.

Fast Facts

OFFICIAL NAME: Kingdom of Belgium
CAPITAL: Brussels

LAND
- Area: 11,787 square miles (30,528 sq km)
- Highest Point: Botrange 2,277 feet (694 m)
- Major Rivers: Meuse, Schelde

PEOPLE
- Population: 10,392,226 (July 2007 estimate)
- Major Cities: Brussels, Antwerp, Ghent
- Official Languages: Dutch, French, German
- Religions: Roman Catholic, Protestantism

GOVERNMENT
- Form: Federal parliamentary democracy under a constitutional monarchy
- Head of State: Monarch
- Head of Government: Prime minister
- Legislature: Bicameral parliament
- Nationhood: October 4, 1830

ECONOMY
- Agricultural Products: Sugar beets, vegetables, fruits, grain, tobacco, beef, veal, pork, milk
- Mining Products: Dolomite, granite, marble, limestone, sandstone
- Manufactured Products: Motor vehicles, chemicals, metals, textiles, glass, petroleum, processed foods and beverages, engineering and metal products
- Money: Euro (1 euro = 100 cents)

Belgium's flag

Belgian one euro coin

Timeline

50s BC	Romans move into present-day Belgium
AD 400s	Frankish tribes invade the Romans
768	Charlemagne comes to power
900s	Local lords gain control of Belgium
1516	Spain takes control of Belgium
1567	Belgians rebel against Spanish control
1713	Austria takes control of Belgium
1789	Belgians revolt against Austrian control
1790s	France gains control of Belgium
1815	France is driven out of Belgium; Belgium becomes part of the Kingdom of the Netherlands
1830	Belgians revolt against the Kingdom of the Netherlands; Belgium gains independence
1831	Leopold I becomes the first king of Belgium
1949	Belgium joins NATO
1951	Belgians help create the European Union
1971	The Belgian Parliament creates the country's three language communities

Through the Years

The earliest people to live in present-day Belgium were Celtic tribes called the Belgae (BEHL-geye). This tribe was probably made up of Celtic and **Germanic** peoples. In the 50s BC, Julius Caesar's Roman army conquered the Belgae. The Romans brought cities, roads, and industry to the region.

In the AD 400s, a Germanic people called the Franks invaded the region. The Frankish Merovingian family made what is now Belgium part of its kingdom. But in the late 600s, the Frankish Carolingian family took over. As part of this family, Charlemagne (SHAHR-luh-mayn) came into power in 768. He eventually made his kingdom into a large empire, with Belgium at the center.

Charlemagne's grandsons split the empire into three kingdoms in 843. But by the 900s, they had lost much of their power. As a result, local lords took control. They provided land and protection to the people they ruled. Towns and cities grew under this system, which lasted for about three centuries.

In 1516, the **Low Countries** fell under Spanish control. Philip II became king of Spain and ruler of the Low Countries in

1556. King Philip was Catholic, and he **persecuted** the **Protestants** in the **Low Countries**. As a result, the people **rebelled** in 1567.

Charlemagne was also called "Charles the Great." He served as king of the Franks from 768 to 814.

By 1579, the **rebellion** had started to weaken. However, King Philip continued to control the southern **provinces**. Meanwhile, **Protestantism** grew stronger in the north. In 1581, present-day Netherlands declared its independence from Spain. Still, fighting continued. Finally in 1648, Spain recognized Netherlands's independence.

Belgium remained under Spanish control until Austria took over in 1713. For a time, Belgium enjoyed political freedom. But in 1781, Austrian ruler Joseph II tried to reform Belgium's administrative, legal, educational, and judicial systems.

In 1789, the Belgians revolted against the Austrians. The Belgians won and created their own country. But Austria soon regained control.

Then in the early 1790s, France invaded Belgium and drove out the Austrians. French rule was harsh. Belgians had little political freedom, and the nobles lost much of their power. In addition, the church was **persecuted**. And, the French language became widespread.

France's emperor Napoléon I was finally defeated in 1815. As a result, Belgium, Netherlands, and Luxembourg became part of the Kingdom of the Netherlands.

King William I gave Belgium little real power in the new kingdom. The official language became Dutch, rather than

Napoléon I met his defeat at the Battle of Waterloo in Belgium on June 18, 1815.

French. And the northern Netherlanders were **Protestant**, while the Belgians were Catholic. Problems concerning politics and education also developed.

The Belgians revolted once again in August 1830. They declared their independence on October 4. In December, the major European countries recognized Belgium's independence. The next year, Leopold I became the first king of independent Belgium. And, the country created a **constitution** and a **parliament**.

Belgium had been **neutral** when it was created. However, the Germans invaded during **World War I**. They used much of Belgium's resources, and the country suffered.

On August 4, 1914, Germany invaded Belgium. By late November, German occupation had spread throughout the country. As a result, Belgium was the site of many battles during World War I.

The Germans again invaded Belgium during **World War II**. Following the war, Belgium's **economy** quickly recovered. The country became a founding member of the **United Nations**. It also joined **NATO** in 1949. King Baudouin I took the throne in 1951. And, Belgians helped create what eventually became the **European Union (EU)**.

In 1971, the Belgian **Parliament** created the three language **culture** communities for Dutch, French, and German speakers. A new **constitution** also established the three regions of Brussels, Flanders, and Wallonia.

The country's economy weakened in the next years. Troubles among the language communities made problem solving difficult. King Baudouin died in 1993. His brother Albert II became king in his place.

King Albert II

Varied Terrain

Located in northwestern Europe, Belgium is only about the size of the state of Maryland. Belgium is bordered by Netherlands in the north and the North Sea in the northwest. France lies to the west and south. Luxembourg is southeast, and Germany is to the east.

Belgium's main land regions are the lowlands near the sea, the Kempenland, the central **plateaus**, and the Ardennes (ahr-DEHN). Lowlands called polders and sand dunes extend across the coastal areas. The polders form a treeless land below sea level that is drained by canals. **Dikes** protect the polders from the sea.

The Kempenland is a slightly higher area to the northeast. There, the land is dry and sandy. Meadows of grass and heather grow there, as well as small pine forests. Marshy areas lie in the west of the region. Reeds and alder trees are also found there.

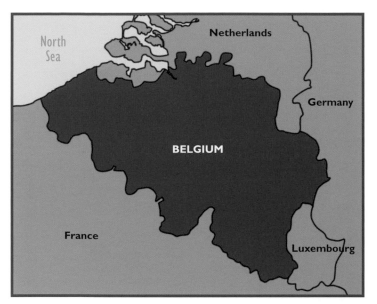

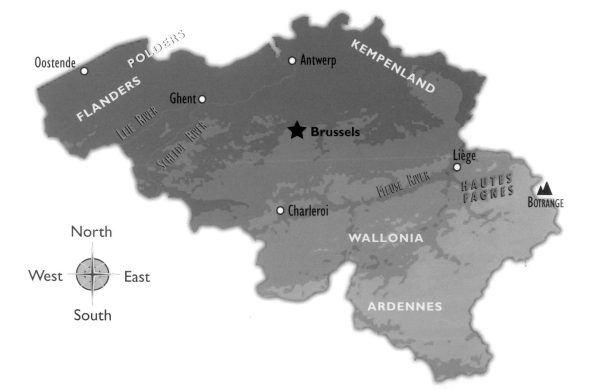

Up from the coast, the land becomes low, rolling hills. The valleys of the central **plateaus** have good farming soil. Many waterways provide water for farms.

The Ardennes is a rocky plateau with thick forests. Botrange (baw-TRAHNZH) is in this area. It is only 2,277 feet (694 m) above sea level. But it is Belgium's highest point.

Two of Belgium's main rivers are the Schelde (SKEHL-duh) and the Meuse (MYOOZ). The Schelde begins in France and flows through western Belgium to the North Sea. This river is one of the country's most important waterways for shipping.

The Meuse River is more eastern. It flows northward from France, through Belgium and Netherlands, and into the North Sea. Many canals connect to the Meuse, allowing shipping and travel throughout Belgium.

Belgium's climate is temperate. The summers are mild. Winters are cool to cold, with frequent rain and snow. In the Ardennes forests, it is cooler year-round.

Rainfall

AVERAGE YEARLY RAINFALL

Inches		Centimeters
Under 20		Under 50
20–40		50–100
40–60		100–150
Over 60		Over 150

Temperature

AVERAGE TEMPERATURE

Fahrenheit		Celsius
Over 65°		Over 18°
54°–65°		12°–18°
32°–54°		0°–12°
21°–32°		-6°–0°
Below 21°		Below -6°

Rain

Winter

North

West — East

South

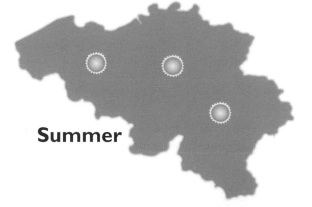

Summer

Wildlife

Thick forests once covered Belgium. Today, much of it is farmland. But, small areas of trees and grasses grow on the remaining open land. There, oak trees are dominant. Other common trees are elms, beeches, and birches. In the Kempenland, large areas of land have been set aside for the planting of birches and pines.

The Ardennes contains a mix of tree types. Both coniferous and deciduous (dih-SIH-juh-wuhs) trees grow in the foothills. There, beeches and oaks are especially common. Higher up, only coniferous trees grow. The Hautes Fagnes (oht FAHN) area in the northeast is a nature reserve. It is covered with peat bogs and some spruce trees.

Many of Belgium's wild animals live in the Ardennes. The most common are wildcats, wild boars, deers, and pheasants. Hamsters and muskrats make their homes in the **basin** to the north. Lapwings, sandpipers, snipes, woodcocks, and other birds live in the lowlands.

Het Zwin Nature Reserve is an important breeding and migrating area for birds. Visitors can spot more than 100 species of birds at this Flanders reserve!

Belgians

Belgians are a mix of **cultures**. Flemings speak Dutch and live in the north. French-speaking Walloons live in the south. And, some German speakers live in eastern Belgium. The country is small and **densely** populated. Most Belgians live in cities and towns. Often, they commute to work.

Belgium's laws allow the people to practice any religion. Most Belgians are Roman Catholic. A small percentage are **Protestant**, while others choose no religion.

Public and private schools are paid for by Belgium's government. More than 90 percent of children attend preschool. All children must attend school from ages 6 to 18. From ages 6 through 11, children attend elementary school. Then in high school, students study basic subjects. They also take technical, **vocational**, or college-preparatory courses.

Belgians enjoy good food. A favorite meal is waterzooi (VAH-tuhr-zoy). This is a stew of fish or chicken, vegetables, herbs, eggs, and cream. Another tasty dish is *stoemp*, which is similar to mashed potatoes. And *frites*, or french fries, served with mayonnaise are popular.

Stoemp

- 2 1/5 pounds potatoes, peeled and cubed
- 2 1/5 pounds carrots, peeled
- 9 ounces bacon, cut in small pieces
- 1 onion, finely chopped
- 1 tablespoon parsley, chopped

- milk
- 1 sprig thyme
- 1 3/4 ounces butter
- salt and pepper

Slice the carrots into thin rounds. Melt butter in a large pan and fry the onion until it is golden. Add carrots, thyme, parsley, and salt and pepper to taste. Cover the vegetables and simmer for 40 minutes. Cook the potatoes in salted water for 20 minutes. Fry the bacon slowly. When everything is ready, mix the vegetables with the potatoes and the bacon. Add milk until it is your preferred consistency. Then, pass the mixture through a vegetable shredder. Season with salt and pepper. Serve very warm with sausages and mustard.

AN IMPORTANT NOTE TO THE CHEF: Always have an adult help with the preparation and cooking of food. Never use kitchen utensils or appliances without adult permission and supervision.

LANGUAGE

English	Dutch	French	German
Good day	Dag (tahk)	Bonjour (bohn-zhoor)	Guten Tag (GOO-tehn tahg)
Good-bye	Tot ziens (toht zeens)	Au revoir (oh vwahr)	Auf Wiedersehen (owf VEE-dehr-zayn)
Please	Alstublieft (AHL-stoo-bleeft)	S'il vous plaît (see voo play)	Bitte (BIHT-teh)
Thank you	Dank u wel (dahnk yoo vehl)	Merci (mehr-see)	Danke (DAHNG-keh)
Yes	Ja (yah)	Oui (wee)	Ja (yah)

Industrious Nation

Belgium has a successful **economy**. Businesses run without much control by the government. About two-thirds of Belgians work in service industries. Of these, education, government, and health care are the most important. Other large employers are retail stores, restaurants, and banks.

Belgians also work in manufacturing. The country's largest industry is the creation of engineering and metal materials, including steel. Other major products are **textiles** such as Belgian lace, carpeting, and **synthetic fibers**. People also make medicines, plastics, and **pesticides**. And, Belgian chocolate is another important product.

Farms in Belgium are small and family owned. However, they produce most of the country's food. Dairy farming and livestock production are the main parts of Belgian agriculture. Farmers grow wheat, barley, potatoes, sugar beets, and other fruits and vegetables. Some farmers also produce large amounts of flowers, especially azaleas.

Coal mining was once a large industry in areas such as the Kempenland. Today, most of this coal has been mined, and production is expensive. However, Belgians still mine dolomite, granite, marble, limestone, and sandstone.

Belgians take great pride in their famous chocolate. This small country produces 172,000 tons (156,000 t) of chocolate each year!

Best-Kept Secrets

The Atomium was built for a 1958 World's Fair. Since then, it has served as a symbol of Brussels.

Brussels is the capital of Belgium. The city and its surrounding areas make up the country's largest population of people. Although Dutch and French are Brussels's official languages, most people there speak French.

This bustling city is the heart of Belgium's political and **economic** activity. Brussels is home to the **EU** and **NATO**. The capital is also known for its fashion. Many small shops are found throughout the city. Celebrated **architecture** and many theaters, museums, and concert halls are located in Brussels, too.

Belgium's largest city, Antwerp, lies on the Schelde River. Antwerp is an important economic center. In fact, it is the world's biggest diamond-trading center. Yet, Antwerp has much

Every two years, about 800,000 begonias are used to fashion a giant flower carpet in Brussels's Grand Place. One hundred gardeners create this masterpiece in less than four hours!

culture to offer. The Cathedral of Notre Dame and the town hall are two of the city's greatest examples of **architecture**.

The country's next largest city is Ghent (GEHNT). Ghent lies on the Leie (LAY-uh) and Schelde rivers and is another important port. It is one of Belgium's oldest cities. Ghent is known for its historic buildings, public squares, and marketplaces. Horticulture and **textiles** are important to this city's **economy**.

Belgian Window

Trains are an important way to get around Belgium. The country has a compact network of about 2,500 miles

In 1835, Belgium built the first railway line in Europe.

(4,000 km) of rail lines. Belgium's **dense** population and its well-lit transportation system make the country shine at night. In fact, astronauts call this the "Belgian Window."

Seaports, inland rivers, and canals provide important travel and shipping routes. Antwerp is the country's busiest seaport.

Zaventem International Airport, near Brussels, is the country's center for air travel. Smaller international airports are located in Antwerp, Oostende, Charleroi (shahr-luh-ROY), and Liège (LYEHZH). From 1923 to 2001,

SABENA was the national airline. However, it no longer operates. Today, Brussels Airlines is Belgium's primary airline.

About 25 daily newspapers keep Belgians informed. People can read the latest news in Dutch or French. There is also one daily newspaper published in German.

Belgians also gather information from radios and televisions. Programs are broadcast in Dutch and French. And, more than 5 million Belgians surf the Internet for information.

British and American newspapers are also easy to obtain in Belgium.

Kingdom of Belgium

Belgium's national government is a **democracy** under a **constitutional monarchy**. The monarch is the head of state. But, the prime minister leads the government and the cabinet called the Council of Ministers. The cabinet has equal numbers of Dutch- and French-speaking members.

The Senate and the Chamber of Representatives make up the Belgian **Parliament**. The Senate has 71 members. Voters choose 40 seats, **provincial** councils appoint 21, and other senators elect 10. The Belgian people elect the 150-member Chamber. Each parliament member serves a four-year term.

Belgium's government provides basic social services and medical insurance for its citizens. In return, all Belgian citizens who are 18 or older must vote in national elections. Citizens who do not vote may have to pay a fine.

Belgian Parliament

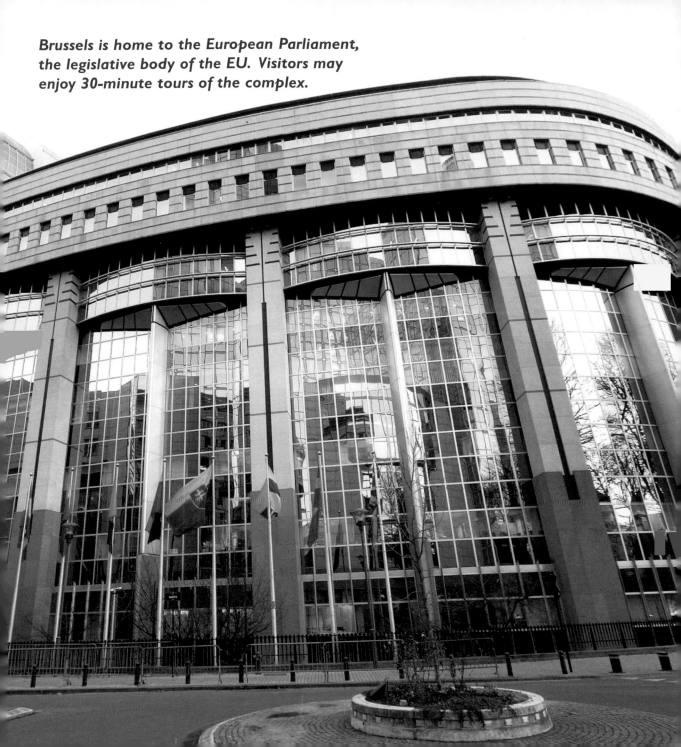

Brussels is home to the European Parliament, the legislative body of the EU. Visitors may enjoy 30-minute tours of the complex.

In the past, the Royal Palace in Brussels was home to the royal family. Today, the king uses the palace as his office. If the Belgian flag is atop the palace, the king is in Belgium.

Belgium has three politically defined regions. They are Flanders in the north, Wallonia in the south, and the Brussels-Capital Region.

Each region has its own prime minister and council. The regional governments are in charge of energy, public works, communications, and **environmental** issues. They manage the spending and the governments of the **provinces**.

There are also three language communities for the Dutch, French, and German speaking peoples. Each community has its own council, which is in charge of **culture**. This includes language, **media**, tourism, sports, museums, and education.

Belgium's ten **provinces** and many cities also have their own governments. A governor and an elected council lead each province. And, each city has a mayor and a town council. These governments are in charge of law enforcement and other local matters.

Belgians are proud of their country.

A Festive Calendar

Holidays are a time for Belgians to come together. The people celebrate National Day on July 21. On this day in 1831, Leopold I took the oath to become Belgium's first king under the new **constitution**. Other national holidays include Labor Day on May 1 and Armistice Day on November 11.

Belgians also celebrate religious holidays such as Easter, Pentecost, All Saint's Day, and Christmas. On December 5, children leave their shoes by the fireplace. The next morning, Saint Nicholas Day, they check to see whether Saint Nicholas has left them sweets or gifts.

Each language community has its own feast day. The Flemings celebrate on July 11. They honor their victory at the Battle of the Golden Spurs in 1302. On September 27, the French community celebrates its feast day. It marks the victory of French patriots over the Dutch army in 1830. The German community's feast day is November 15.

May 8 is the Brussels-Capital Region's feast day. And, the Wallonia Region celebrates its feast day on the third Sunday in September.

One of Belgium's most famous celebrations is Carnival in the town of Binche. Gilles, or males who were born and raised in Binche, dress in clownlike costumes. They parade through the city streets and hand out oranges.

Many cities and towns have their own festivals as well. Whatever the occasion, Belgians celebrate with costumes, food, and sporting events.

Art and Recreation

Antwerp's Cathedral of Our Lady is Belgium's largest church.
It houses three works by Belgian artist Peter Paul Rubens.

Belgian history is rich with the arts. The people preserve this history in museums. Palaces, opera houses, theaters, and concert halls also provide ways to enjoy Belgian traditions.

Many painters came from Belgium. René Magritte and Paul Delvaux painted **surrealist** works in the early 1900s. Other great Flemish artists include Jan van Eyck. Van Eyck painted in the 1400s and became known for his portraits.

Belgium has been the birthplace of several talented musicians as well. These include César Franck, who pushed the limits of classical music. Adolphe Sax created the first saxophone. This instrument became a favorite among jazz musicians. Today, Jean "Toots" Thielemans continues to make jazz music popular worldwide.

Belgium's arts includes respected literature. Maurice Maeterlinck became famous for his plays, including *The Blue Bird*. In 1911, Maeterlinck won the **Nobel Prize** for Literature.

Many Belgians love jazz music. Belgium hosts numerous jazz festivals throughout the year.

Many Belgian comics have become known throughout the world. Two familiar ones are the *Smurfs* by Pierre "Peyo" Culliford and *Tintin* by Georges "Hergé" Rémi.

Belgian films are made with small budgets. However, some films have received awards at the Cannes (KAWN) Film Festival in France. Two of the most famous Belgian film directors are Luc and Jean-Pierre Dardenne.

To relax, many Belgians play sports. As in most European countries, soccer is quite popular. Bicycling is also loved in Belgium. Other popular sports include tennis, running, golf, and sailing.

Good food is also a strong part of Belgian **culture**. People regularly

The Grottes de Han, or Caves of Han, are located in the Ardennes region. Visitors should bring a jacket. These caves are only about 54 degrees Fahrenheit (12°C).

dine at fine restaurants and cafés. There, they can sample many of Belgium's famous beers.

For everyday recreation, Belgians visit parks scattered throughout the cities. For longer vacations, many people head to the North Sea or the Ardennes. Anyone can experience rich **culture**, fine dining, and serious sports in Belgium!

Outdoor cafés offer good people watching and some of Belgium's gourmet food.

Glossary

architecture - the art of planning and designing buildings.

basin - the entire region of land drained by a river and its tributaries.

constitution - the laws that govern a country.

constitutional monarchy - a form of government ruled by a monarch who must follow the laws of a constitution.

culture - the customs, arts, and tools of a nation or people at a certain time.

democracy - a governmental system in which the people vote on how to run their country.

dense - having many people in a small area.

dike - a bank or a barrier constructed to control or confine water.

economy - the way a nation uses its money, goods, and natural resources.

environment - all the surroundings that affect the growth and well-being of a living thing.

European Union (EU) - an organization of European countries that works toward political, economic, governmental, and social unity.

Germanic - of people of northwestern Europe in the Middle Ages.

Low Countries - a region in Western Europe that borders the North Sea and includes modern-day Belgium, Luxembourg, and Netherlands.

media - communication companies, such as the news media.

NATO - North Atlantic Treaty Organization. A group formed by the United States, Canada, and some European countries in 1949. It tries to create peace among its nations and protect them from common enemies.

neutral - not taking sides in a conflict.

Nobel Prize - an award for someone who has made outstanding achievements in his or her field of study.

parliament - the highest lawmaking body of some governments.

persecute - to harass someone because of his or her origin, religion, or beliefs.

pesticide - a chemical used to kill insects.

plateau - a raised area of flat land.

Protestant - a Christian who does not belong to the Catholic Church.

province - a geographical or governmental division of a country.

rebellion - an armed resistance or defiance of a government. To rebel is to disobey an authority or the government.

surrealist - of or relating to a modern art movement featuring unexpected arrangements and distorted images.

synthetic fiber - any fiber developed by chemical processes from natural substances such as petroleum and coal. Rayon and nylon are well-known synthetic fibers.

textile - a woven fabric or cloth.

United Nations - a group of nations formed in 1945. Its goals are peace, human rights, security, and social and economic development.

vocational - relating to training in a skill or a trade to be pursued as a career.

World War I - from 1914 to 1918, fought in Europe. Great Britain, France, Russia, the United States, and their allies were on one side. Germany, Austria-Hungary, and their allies were on the other side.

World War II - from 1939 to 1945, fought in Europe, Asia, and Africa. Great Britain, France, the United States, the Soviet Union, and their allies were on one side. Germany, Italy, Japan, and their allies were on the other side.

Web Sites

To learn more about Belgium, visit ABDO Publishing Company on the World Wide Web at **www.abdopublishing.com**. Web sites about Belgium are featured on our Book Links page. These links are routinely monitored and updated to provide the most current information available.

Index